CONCRETE GIANTS OF ARDYNE POINT

JAMES CARRON

Amenta Publishing

CONCRETE GIANTS OF ARDYNE POINT

By James Carron

First published 2024 by Amenta Publishing

Copyright © James Carron 2024

ISBN 9798345501009

The right of James Carron to be identified as the author of this work has been asserted by him in accordance with the Copyright, Designs and Patents Act 1988.

All rights reserved. No part of this publication may be reproduced, stored in a retrieval system, or transmitted in any form, or by any means, electronic, mechanical, photocopying, recording or otherwise, without permission in writing from the publisher.

Front cover – Brent Charlie concrete gravity base platform under construction at Ardyne Point

Rear cover – Frigg TP1 under construction in Loch Striven (top) and an aerial view of the yard and its dry docks (below)

The *Brent Charlie* platform under construction at Ardyne Point for Shell/Esso in 1977 – British Geological Survey

The *Cormorant Alpha* platform under construction at Ardyne Point for Shell/Esso in 1977 – British Geological Survey

Introduction

In the heady early days of North Sea oil exploration, the civil engineering firm of Sir Robert McAlpine enjoyed success where many others failed. Following the discovery of large reserves of oil and gas under the North Sea in 1970, Britain's Labour government and a plethora of private companies invested heavily in new yards designed to build the platforms necessary to extract this fresh resource. It was a time of frenetic activity in the face of stiff competition, particularly from Norway.

With a single platform costing up to £60 million, it was a lucrative business to be in and, by 1974, a dozen British firms were battling for rig orders. Securing just one platform could create work for thousands of men for up to three years, at a time when unemployment was high in the UK, and bring in healthy profits.

It was also a time of great uncertainty, primarily over which type of rigs operators would go for. On one side of the line were traditional steel platforms. On the other, the more costly concrete gravity platforms.

Early entrants included Highland Fabricators, a consortium set up by Brown & Root and Wimpey, which carved out a graving dock at Nigg Bay on the Cromarty Firth and was setting to work on the first two steel platforms for BP's Forties field.

Redpath Dorman Long moved into a disused coastal colliery site at Methil, in Fife, to build a steel platform for Shell/Esso's Auk field and the company later won the contract for the first platform for Shell's giant Brent field.

The American firm of J Ray McDermott Inc had a site at Ardersier, near Inverness, and Mid-Continental Supply Company (UK) Ltd developed one upstream from Nigg at Dalmore. Approval was also given to Brital Marine Ltd for a yard at

Evanton and CBI Constructors Ltd for platform building at Dunnet Bay, near Thurso.

With all this frantic activity, a note of caution was soon sounded by the International Management and Engineering Group whose study of potential benefits to industry from offshore oil and gas developments, commissioned by the Department of Trade and Industry, suggested the entry of further firms into the sector could create an undesirable level of over-capacity. The warning, however, was not heeded and at least four more companies joined the fray.

Taylor Woodrow Construction Ltd secured a site at Alness, north of Inverness, and Anglo-Dutch Offshore Concrete (Andoc) at Burntisland, in Fife. John Mowlem & Company Ltd, dropped plans for a yard on Loch Broom, near Ullapool, but joined forces with Taylor Woodrow to seek permission for a yard at Drumbuie, on Loch Carron. The controversial application was rejected after a public outcry over the impact it would have on the landscape and local communities led to a public inquiry.

All of the initial UK contracts awarded by the oil companies were for traditional steel platforms. The base – known as the jacket – was usually constructed on its side in a coastal yard. Once complete, the structure was floated out horizontally to its deep-sea location, tipped up and sunk vertically to the seabed where the legs were secured with piles. A deck would then be attached to the top. The first successful construction sites were all on the east coast of Scotland, closer to the oil fields.

While steel rigs were, at that time, industry standard around the world, concrete was viewed as a viable alternative. The Norwegians pioneered the technology, developing the first prototype – a concrete floatable platform – in 1970. The nation's engineers had experience in concrete construction techniques, having built numerous dams using the material, and the country's fjords offered the deep water necessary for platform building.

Shortly after oil was discovered in the North Sea, the country's leading contractors joined forces to create Norwegian Contractors in 1973 to take advantage of the new opportunities. They developed Condeep, a concrete gravity-based platform that would stand securely on the seabed by the force of its weight alone.

Built in stages, the initial work was undertaken in a dry dock. Once the concrete base was complete, the dock was flooded and the structure floated into deeper water where the legs were constructed upwards.

Once complete, the base, ballasted down in the water, would be towed vertically to its drilling location and lowered on to the seabed. Although more expensive to build, concrete platforms were cheaper to install, more resilient to rough seas, and could be pre-loaded with equipment.

North Sea oil extraction and concrete platforms were both in their infancy and, while the oil companies remained cautious about concrete, it was not long before the British government decided it was the way forward.

Debating the Offshore Petroleum Development (Scotland) Bill – new legislation designed to facilitate and control developments in the North Sea oil and gas industry – in November 1974, Minister of State at the Scottish Office Bruce Millan told the House of Commons that the newly discovered oil resources of the North Sea must be exploited quickly for the nation's economic benefit.

Britain in the 1970s was at an economic low, crippled by high unemployment, frequent strikes, high inflation, the three-day week, and energy shortages, brought on by a rise in the cost of imported oil due to the Arab Israeli war in the Middle East.

Millan stated: 'The establishment of a concrete platform construction industry in Scotland is crucial to the exploitation of oil in the North Sea. It is very much bound up with the question of getting oil out as quickly as possible because the work involved will be an important source of jobs and prosperity for the people of Scotland. I hope that nobody will underemphasise the importance of concrete platform construction and other oil-related activities from that point of view.'

The Scottish Office estimated 'a minimum of 50' platforms would be required over the next 10 years for the British sector of the North Sea, suggesting as many as 200 may ultimately be needed. By creating nationalised yards, the government hoped to provide the infrastructure necessary while at the same time preventing over-supply and the destruction of areas of natural beauty in the West Highlands in the rush to build these new platforms.

Millan acknowledged that good coastal construction sites were scarce and tended to be in socially and environmentally sensitive areas.

'Public ownership provides the right mechanism to deal effectively with the situation. It enables the maximum use to be made of sites and avoids proliferation,' he continued.

'This is an important point to emphasise at present when concern is being expressed in some quarters that we are at risk of having too many platform construction sites. I do not think that there is a risk of this, but to the extent that people have fears on this score I hope that the Bill will help to put them at rest.

'Public ownership also emphasises to oil companies and platform builders the Government's intention that sites will be available in good time for the designs favoured by the operators. It ensures that only the requisite amount of infrastructure is provided so that there is not waste. Finally, it enables strict control to be exercised over developments and ensures the ultimate restoration or adaptation of the sites.'

Scotland's deep west coast sea lochs were perfect for the much-vaunted concrete platforms and proposals for more yards soon followed. John Howard & Company Ltd and the French firm

Doris Engineering successfully applied for permission to build concrete platforms on Loch Kishorn, sliding in almost unnoticed following the abandonment of the nearby Drumbuie project.

Costain Civil Engineering Ltd promoted plans for a yard at Hunterston, on the Firth of Clyde; Balfour Beatty for Finnart Bay, on Loch Long; and Anglo-Dutch consortium Subtank Constructors (UK) Ltd identified Portavadie, on Loch Fyne, as their preferred option.

It therefore came as something of a blow to both the government and the British firms when orders for the North Sea's first three concrete platforms were awarded to Norwegian firms.

In 1973, Phillips Petroleum took delivery of the 80,000-tonne concrete *Ekofisk 2/4T* platform, the world's first concrete structure for the offshore oil industry. Built in Stavanger in 1971-73, the Doris type structure (a single column with a perforated breakwater wall around it), which became operational on January 3, 1974, was a giant storage tank that held up to a million barrels of crude oil ahead of its loading on to tankers for shipping to shore.

On July 20, 1973, Mobil commissioned a Condeep platform – *Beryl Alpha* – for its Beryl field from Hoyer-Ellefsen, of Stavanger, and Shell followed suit, ordering a Condeep from Hoyer-Ellefsen – *Brent Bravo* – for the Brent field. Both fields lay in the UK sector, which made the loss of orders to Norway a bitter pill to swallow.

John Mowlem & Company Ltd held the licence to build Condeep platforms in the UK but had so far failed to find a construction site. After losing Loch Broom and Drumbuie, the firm adapted its design and turned its attention to Macringan's Point, Campbeltown, winning government support and finally securing planning consent.

To be in the running for orders, a company had to first either design a concrete platform or secure the rights to one and then locate and build a suitable site where the structure could take shape. Both elements were submitted for government approval. Under the new Bill, the government, with the help of independent consultants, was able to identify platform designs which were likely to be commercially viable and then match them to sites.

Amid all this, the long-established civil engineering firm of Sir Robert McAlpine & Sons Ltd, in partnership with French platform designers Sea Tank Company, stole a march on their competitors, securing their first order for Scotland months before the other yards were ready. McAlpine had a long history of building with concrete, most notably the Glenfinnan railway viaduct on the line between Fort William and Mallaig, in the West Highlands, and the Blackwater Reservoir dam, constructed in the early 1900s for the British Aluminium Company at Kinlochleven.

In January 1974, the McAlpine partnership signed a contract with the French company Elf to build *Frigg TP1*. The unit was a Treatment Platform designed to process gas from two neighbouring platforms before it was piped ashore. This was swiftly followed by orders for two more concrete gravity platforms for Shell/Esso's Brent and Cormorant fields. The latter, when complete, was briefly the world's largest manmade moveable structure.

But even at that early stage there were concerns that Britain was falling behind other countries, Norway in particular, having secured only £74 million of the £480 million being invested in North Sea infrastructure.

McAlpine's men had been secretly scouting sites in Cowal for a concrete platform yard since 1972. Allowing the media and local communities to focus on a speculative American plan for a rig yard at Ardyne Point, the firm's surveyors mapped out a site and bought or leased the land it needed under a cloak of confidentiality.

McAlpine finally revealed its plans in Glasgow in December 1973, announcing that, subject to planning approval and working with the Sea Tank Company, it intended to start work on its first concrete platform early the following year, employing a peak workforce of 400 men. *The Scotsman* reported in January 1974 that the 'UK's first construction site for gigantic oil and gas platforms' was being carved out of 40 acres of land, work progressing 'seven days a week' on two massive dry docks.

Planning permission was granted without fuss and a dry dock and wharfs were constructed at Ardyne Point, near Toward, on Loch Striven. As the project progressed, permission was promptly sought to extend the wharf and carve out a second and then a third basin. In all, a million cubic metres of earth and rock were excavated from the Loch Striven shoreline and mounded up to create an artificial hill.

Given the huge demand placed on onshore prefabrication sites, and the significance of the water depths available to constructors for fabricating and towing these giant structures near to the shore, there were a wide variety of different concrete gravity base designs on the market, each constrained by the geography and conditions of the construction site. It therefore proved impossible to create an optimized design suitable to be built at all available sites, although the construction process was the same.

Concrete gravity platforms were built in a tapered shape, with as much of the mass and bulk concentrated as close as possible to the seabed. Ideally, the platform was constructed close to the shore, and the topside facilities attached in a sheltered deeper water site before the offshore tow began.

Layers of concrete reinforced with steel would be built up to create domed caissons on a base that would eventually sit on the seabed. Constructed in drydock, these cassions contained tanks that, during the construction and installation phases, would be filled with ballast to lower the structure in the water and eventually submerge the base and much of the legs in the North Sea. Thereafter they would be used as reservoirs for oil or gas storage.

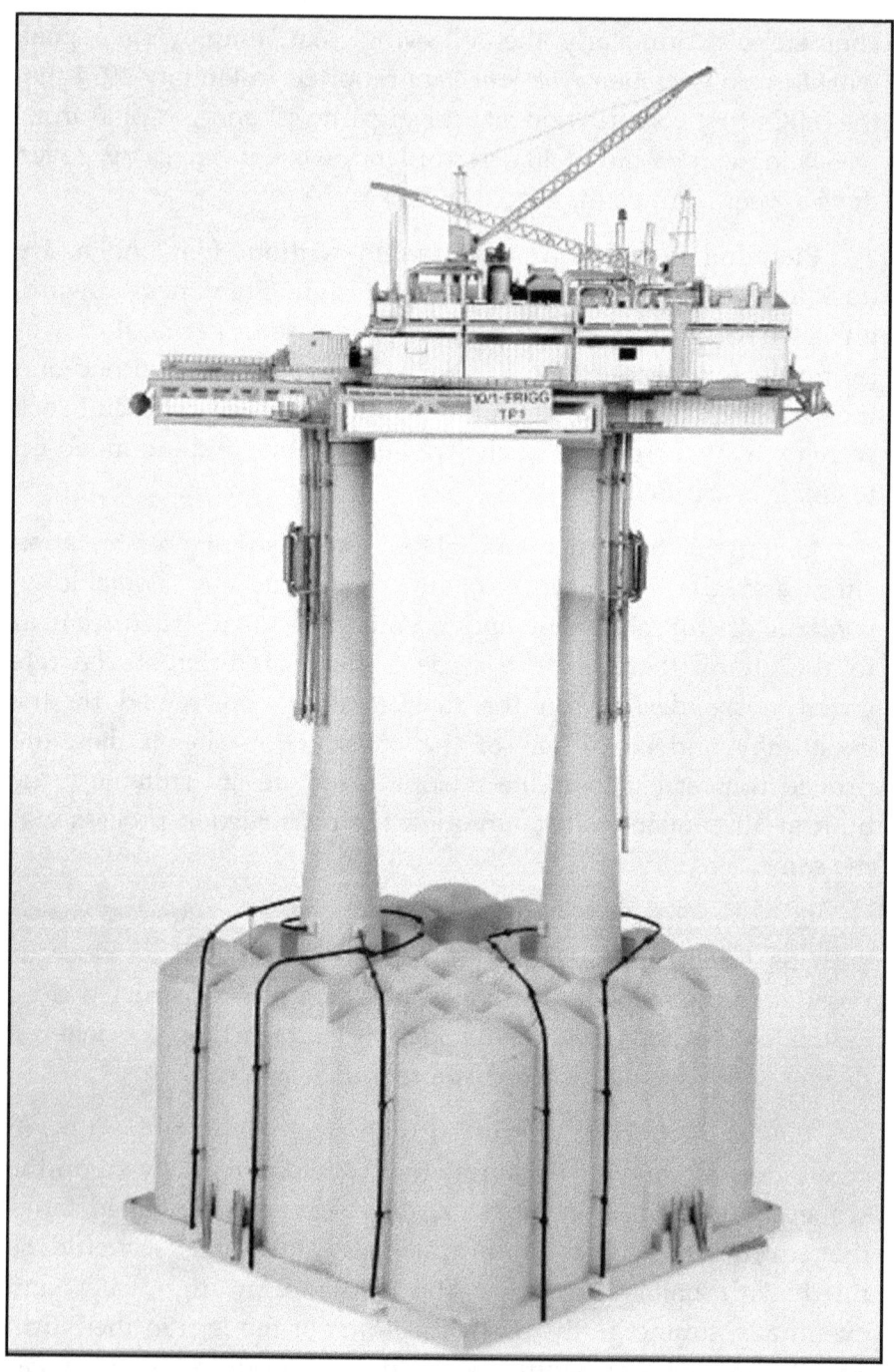

Model of the *Frigg TP1* platform built for Elf, showing the concrete base and legs – Norwegian Petroleum Museum

The 166,000 tonne *Frigg TP1* platform had 25 44-metre high cylindrical caissons arranged into a square at its base from which two 133-metre-high legs extended upwards.

Once the base was finished, the dock would be flooded, the gate removed, and the section floated out into the loch. The structure would then be lowered in the water, allowing the towering legs to be erected on top of it. Work would be undertaken both from a barge and on land where sections could be prefabricated before being shipped out.

Thereafter the completed platform would be moved to its final location by a fleet of ocean-going tugs. The journey would have been a lengthy one and would have first involved travelling south via the Firth of Clyde, rounding the southern tip of the Kintyre peninsula and Isle of Jura before heading north through the Irish Channel, up the west coast of Scotland and through the Pentland Firth to the North Sea.

When the platform reached its offshore location, the caissons in the base would be water ballasted, lowered down and landed on the seabed, the platform installed and operational within a matter of days, a huge benefit in harsh areas of the North Sea with only short windows of fair weather.

In addition to performing well in rough seas, concrete platforms were more resistant to corrosion than their steel counterparts.

Handling such large and heavy concrete structures, particularly when they were floating in the sea, was not without its complications, as the case of the Norwegian-built *Sleipner A* platform proved. During tests, one of the Condeep platform's 24 base cells cracked and sprang a leak as it was being lowered in the water and the whole structure sank in a Norwegian fjord. Subsequent investigations highlighted a design flaw; as the water pressure increased at depth, the walls failed and cracked.

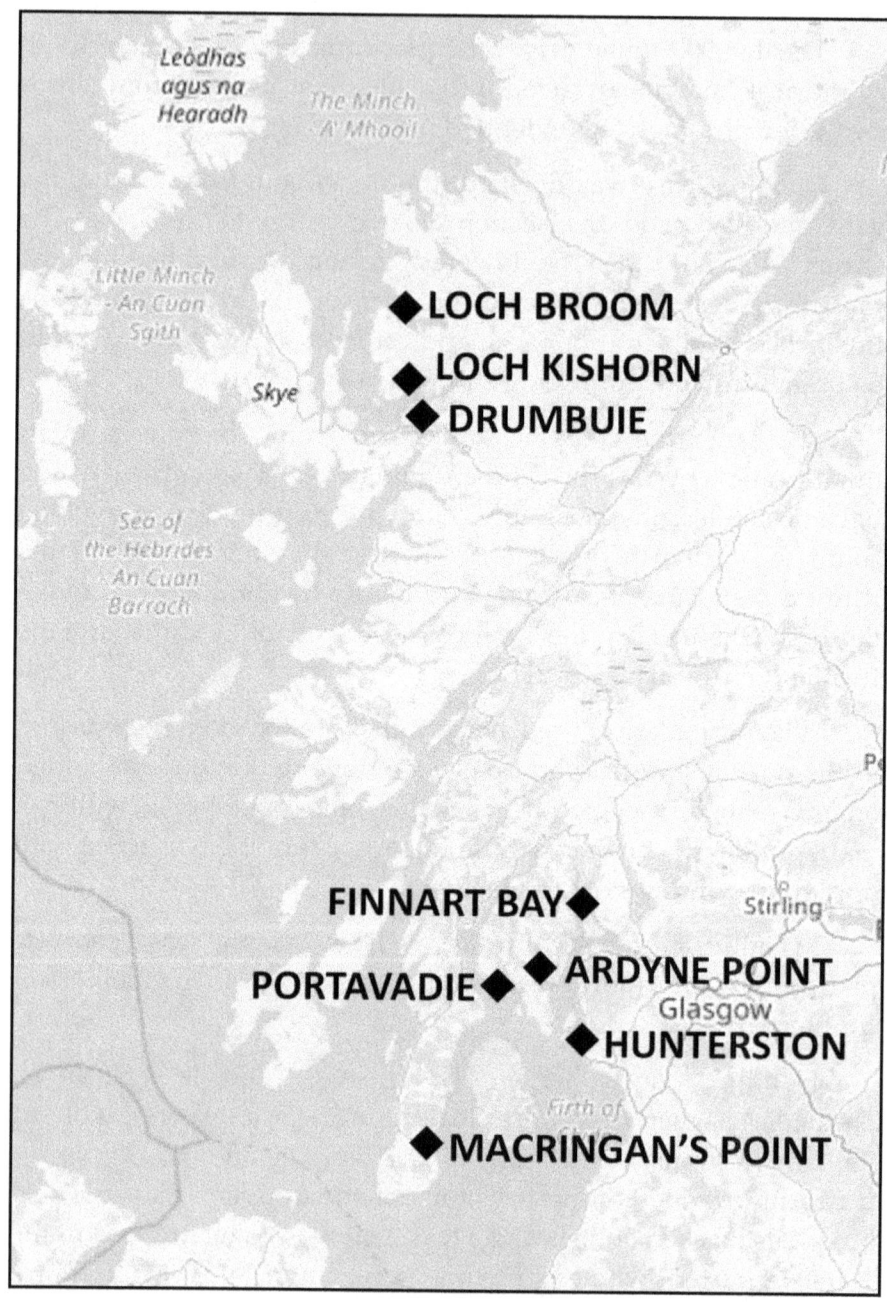

Overview map showing locations of proposed and actual concrete gravity base construction sites in western Scotland

Norway was not the only country benefitting in the British sector of the North Sea. The arrival of civil engineering structures from France, Sweden and the Netherlands all added fuel to the fire of those who claimed that not enough was being done by the British government.

There were concerns that ministers had deferred matters relating to North Sea oil over the summer of 1974 and only really got to grips with the issue in the latter part of the year when the Offshore Petroleum Development (Scotland) Bill was passing through the House of Commons.

On January 11, 1975, the government authorising three more sites in Scotland for the construction of concrete production platforms – one at Macringan's Point, Campbeltown, to be operated by Mowlem-Taylor Offshore, one at Portavadie on Loch Fyne, for Sea Platform Constructors (Scotland), and the third at Hunterston, on the Clyde estuary, for the Andoc group. This meant that six of the seven preferred platform designs identified by the Department of Energy in August now had sites available for construction.

The Scottish Office wanted float-outs from all three yards in 1977 and to aid this it agreed to fund the construction of the yards at Portavadie and Hunterston. At the time there was speculation Portavadie was in the running for a Shell contract to build a platform for the Brent field.

Bruce Millan said the government would take all three sites into public ownership to ensure that there was no delay in development, adding that he had 'no worries' about the selected companies obtaining orders for platforms.

Other platform builders remained equally enthusiastic with plans for yet another west coast yard – this time at Portkil Bay, Dunbartonshire – being put forward by civil engineering firm John Laing. The company was already building steel rigs at a former shipyard in Hartlepool and, while plans for the concrete platform project at Portkil were approved by the local council, they were called in by the government.

As work at Portavadie began, negotiations continued between the government and John Mowlem & Company Ltd/Mowlem Taylor and Andoc to agree terms for developing Macringan's Point at Campbeltown and Hunterston respectively. An Offshore Supplies Office spokesman said the quick agreement reached underlined the Government's interest in rapid development of the sites.

The move concentrated platform construction in the waters of south-west Scotland, closer to the Clyde estuary and centres of population like Glasgow, from where a strong labour force could be sourced and where employment opportunities were badly needed.

Between 1975 and 1978, the government spent £22.8 million on the development of the yards at Portavadie and Hunterston, and that figure had risen to £29.2 million by 1986.

The government pressed ahead with its plans to develop Loch Fyne as a centre for deep-water oil platform construction. *The Glasgow Herald* reported on May 27, 1975, that the loch was to be Scotland's first sea-designated area for platform work.

Clyde Port Authority would issue licences to builders to carry out work on the open water. The yard at Ardyne Point, operated by McAlpine, was provisionally allocated two of the four platform moorings available while the third, at Eilean Buidhe, was issued to Sea Platform Constructors at Portavadie. The fourth remained unallocated.

While other sites struggled to secure orders, McAlpine, already busy on *Frigg TP1*, had the capacity to produce multiple platforms – as many as six – at the same time, and the Ardyne Point yard followed this up with two more concrete platforms. In 1974 work began on *Brent Charlie* for Shell/Esso, one of four platforms in Shell UK's Brent oilfield, located to the east of

Shetland. The third contract was for *Cormorant Alpha*, to be located in the East Shetland Basin, 100 miles northeast of Shetland, again for Shell/Esso.

The workforce rose quickly from the original 400 estimate to around 3000 at the peak of the yard's productivity. Around 350 men were billeted to a navvy camp on site, a further 200 came from the local area and hundreds more arrived daily on scheduled and chartered ferries from Glasgow, Clydeside, Ayrshire and the neighbouring island of Bute.

While McAlpine's were busy constructing multiple platforms at Ardyne Point, Balfour Beatty Construction (Scotland) Ltd applied for permission to open a yard at nearby Finnart Bay on Loch Long, prompting outrage from residents who feared their homes would be lost to the development. The plans were subsequently scrapped.

Despite the early optimism, only four concrete platforms were built in Scotland for the North Sea, three of them at Ardyne Point. McAlpine Sea Tank were undoubtedly winners in the brief window of concrete platform construction in Scotland, snatching what work there was from competitors who were not yet even ready to pour their first drop of concrete. They were up and running before the government had a chance to implement its nationalised yard scheme. Timing, it appears, was everything. With the industry opting for less expensive and more flexible steel rigs, the estimated demand for concrete platforms was revised in 1976 from over 60 to just four orders a year, but no more materialised.

Concrete platforms were being manufactured for the North Sea at the rate of one or two a year throughout the 1970s, 80s and 90s but most of the work was being done in Norway. Its yards produced 17 concrete gravity base structures for the North Sea between 1973 and 1995. Most of them were Condeeps, the largest being *Troll A*, completed in 1995 for Shell.

McAlpine Sea Tank devised a range of innovative concrete barges and subsea installations in a bid to save the Ardyne Point yard which, with the departure of the last of the three platforms, was being run on a care and maintenance basis by 1978. But, after just four years of operation, the company abandoned the site.

Brent Charlie under construction for Shell/Esso in Loch Striven in 1977 – McAlpine Sea Tank

1

With the first order for a concrete platform still to be placed, Sir Robert McAlpine & Sons Ltd was, during the summer of 1973, busy preparing a lochside site at Ardyne Point for construction work. The firm envisaged employing some 400 people at the remote location, predicting it would take around 16 months to complete each platform. Despite the remote location, the company did not anticipate any issues in finding a sufficiently large and suitably skilled workforce and planned to employ men already working on its contracts to the south which were coming to an end. Most would be shipped in on specially chartered ferries while others would be accommodated in an onsite camp, and some would be drawn from the local community.

The East Cowal peninsula was first linked to platform construction in 1972 when a letter to the editor of the *Dunoon Observer* newspaper revealed that an American firm had surveyed Ardyne Point with a view to opening a yard for the construction of 'oil rig legs'. However, while rumour and conjecture of an American invasion quickly spread, no one knew that Robert McAlpine had already quietly drawn up preliminary plans for the point.

Early in 1972, company surveyors visited, mapped out the proposed site and made confidential offers to local farmers and landowners to buy the land it needed. It was not until November of that year that the news finally broke. *The Daily Record* reported on November 4, 1972, that Sir Robert McAlpine & Sons Ltd, along with its French partner, Sea Tank, planned to open a new yard – the first in the west of Scotland – to build concrete offshore platforms. It confirmed it would be located at Ardyne Point and that the proposals were already at an advanced stage. The news was also reported by the local Press and, while a surprise to Cowal residents, the response was generally muted.

In December, the company, alongside Sea Tank, outlined the plans more fully at a three-day conference held in the Excelsior Hotel, at Glasgow Airport. The company stated: 'Subject to planning approval McAlpine intend commencing production on the first concrete drilling platform at Ardyne Point, Toward, early in 1973, employing a peak workforce of 400 men in an area where unemployment is at a distressingly high level.'

The company was clearly confident it would gain approval for the project. It had bought the land and, in November 1972 – four months before the planning application was decided – piles of steel stacked at the entrance to the site were pictured in a local newspaper.

There was some opposition, mainly in the form of well-attended protest meetings held in Toward, but these were targeted at another proposed yard at Ardyne Point, one mooted by the civil engineering firm of Peter Lind & Company Ltd. As a result, the McAlpine project progressed with little resistance.

The company was already busy touting designs for platforms that could be used on the Frigg field, which straddled the border between the British and Norwegian sectors of the North Sea and was open to orders from companies operating either side of the line.

Through its partnership with the Paris-based Sea Tank Company, it held the UK rights to build the Seatank platform and it and Ingeniør Thor Furuholmen, one of the largest construction companies in Norway at the time, stood to share all the construction contracts in the North Sea for this design of platform.

Seatank was a caisson and tower arrangement with 36 cylindrical cells arranged in a square (six per side) at its base. Four towers extended upwards from four of the cells. Seatank was designed as a drilling, production, and storage platform. It could store 650,000 to a million barrels of crude oil, could stand in 140 metres of water, and, theoretically at least, could be refloated and moved by its operator. Gravity was intended as the sole means of ensuring stability although the base had a three-metre metal skirt that would penetrate the seabed to prevent sideways movement.

Permission for the yard at Ardyne Point was granted by Secretary of State for Scotland, Gordon Campbell, on March 6, 1973, and formal approval by Argyll County Council followed. Campbell granted the application with stringent conditions, including a requirement to reinstate the land once platform construction operations ceased. He expressed his hope that allowing development here would prevent the landscape of the west coast being damaged by a proliferation of yards and hinted that he might be able to accept another yard at Ardyne, which possessed significant benefits in terms of its proximity of deep water to flat land and a reasonable pool of labour.

In its application, to alleviate traffic concerns, McAlpine undertook to bring in the bulk of raw materials by sea and to ferry in workers. The company also dismissed claims made by firms seeking to locate yards further north that the water depths around the Clyde were insufficient to enable structures to be towed out to sea. It argued that its consultants had advised that it was possible to tow out structures suitable for use at depths of 150 metres or more.

With applications for platform yards around the west coast of Scotland being regularly submitted, it became clear in 1973/74 that the government appeared to favour those on and around the Firth of Clyde as a way of reducing landscape damage to the West Highlands. Plans for a yard at Drumbuie in Wester Ross were rejected following a planning inquiry prompted by complaints from local residents, although proposals for one across the water at Kishorn were approved. The government, however, ended up backing two on the Clyde, one at Portavadie and a second at Hunterston.

Strathclyde Industrial Development advertised heavily in offshore journals, boasting the region as the 'launch platform to success in North Sea Oil' in full page ads and promoting the region's four sites for the manufacture of platforms – Ardyne Point, Campbeltown, Portavadie and Hunterston.

Ardyne Point is a headland on the Cowal peninsula in Argyll & Bute. It lies at the southern end of Loch Striven, across the water from the Isle of Bute, and is a 10-mile drive south from the town of Dunoon, via the village of Toward. Prior to the arrival of the construction yard, Ardyne Point was a flat piece of coastal farmland. However, this peaceful strip of lochside grazing was not completely undeveloped. In the 1960s, the Loch Striven Oil Fuel Depot was constructed to the north of the proposed platform site to serve as a diesel and aviation fuel storage depot for the Royal Navy and NATO vessels. The site was for a time designated as a 'Z-Berth', where nuclear powered vessels were permitted to moor.

Indeed, Loch Striven has an interesting history, much of it connected to the military. During the Second World War, the loch was used for training sub-mariners, particularly those who operated the top-secret X-Craft, a midget submarine built for the Royal Navy between 1943 and 1944. Ardtarig House, an Edwardian shooting lodge near the head of the loch, and the Kyles Hydro Hotel, in Port Bannatyne, served as their bases.

The loch was also used for tests of *Highball*, a smaller version of the Barnes Wallis bouncing bomb, *Upkeep*, designed for use against battleships. The bombs were intended to be delivered by smaller and lighter aircraft and would be deployed using Mosquito fighter bombers of 618 Squadron, based at RAF Turnberry, in Ayrshire. No explosives were used during the testing phase which was mainly aimed at improving the precision of the delivery. A redundant French First World War battleship, *Courbet*, was moored in the loch as the target and nets were draped underneath, designed to catch the bombs so that they could be recovered easily. An underwater archaeological investigation conducted in 2010 found evidence of an anchor chain and several *Highball* devices on the bottom of the loch.

Loch Striven was later used as a test range for submarines. In 1954, British submarine *HMS Templar*, a veteran of the Second World War, was sunk in the loch for use as a target. Four years later she was salvaged and taken to Troon where she was scrapped.

In more recent times, the loch has served as a parking lot for laid up vessels; in the 1970s and 1980s, at least half a dozen lay at anchor in Loch Striven. They included two gas tankers, rendered obsolete upon competition of construction in 1978 by the oil crisis, which stayed there for over a decade before finally being bought by Shell in 1989 and recommissioned. In 2009, due to a downturn in world trade, six Maersk containerships were laid up on the loch, moored in a raft formation.

McAlpine initially secured 40 acres of the ground and soon moved men and machinery on to the site. With an initial workforce of around 70, the first job was to carve out the two massive drydocks where platform construction would commence. These were square in shape and temporary coffer dams of earth and rock were mounded over the mouths of each to prevent the ingress of water from the loch. The basins each measured approximately 150 x 180 metres at their bases and were around 20 metres deep. They could each comfortably accommodate a football pitch with room to spare.

On January 26, 1974, *The Scotsman* reported: 'A sea of mud being slapped into place by giant crawler tractors is all that indicates the UK's first construction site for giant concrete oil and gas platforms is being carved out of 40 acres of Argyll land at Ardyne Point.

'Work drives ahead seven days a week on forming two massive dry docks in which 550-foot-high platforms destined for harsh conditions in the North Sea will rise. Worth a total of £37 million, the first of the two platforms should be dwarfing the peninsula within 12 months.'

Over a million cubic feet of earth was moved in a period of seven months as the basins were scooped out, coastal land was reclaimed, and ground was flattened to accommodate the new camp.

With two contracts in the bag and a tight schedule, the firm intended to begin work on the larger and more complicated of the projects, the *Brent Charlie* platform for Shell/Esso, in March 1974 before floating it out in the summer. The second platform, *Frigg TP1*, would commence construction in the neighbouring dry dock a month later.

Riding an early wave of success, in September 1974, the company announced that it had secured a third order, a deal to build a platform for the Cormorant oilfield, east of the Shetlands. In August 1974 the company was successful in its application for planning permission to expand the yard to around 100 acres and carve out a third dry dock. Despite some vocal local opposition, consent was given by the Secretary of State.

While local opposition was initially mooted, it became more vociferous as McAlpine unveiled proposals to extend the yard along the shoreline, in part to cope with the vast scale of the construction projects and in part to keep rivals Lind out. Some locals were benefitting from the influx of workers, renting rooms and flats, or selling them their houses, while others were noticing the steady increase in lorries trundling along the road from Dunoon to Toward and the large numbers of Glaswegian navvies arriving daily on the ferries. There was concern about the expanding nature of the project; first one dry dock, then two with a third in the offing. There was also anger that McAlpine appeared to be exceeding the scope of its original planning application, and the county council appointed an Enforcement Officer for the Ardyne project in April 1974. Assurances were also sought that when platform construction began, priority would be given to local labour.

Inland from the dry docks, on a platform of concrete, McAlpine created a temporary encampment to service the yard. Primarily portable cabins, this included a navvy camp with basic accommodation and facilities for some 350 workers who would live on site. There was also a large canteen, offices and stores.

The opening of the yard was not without problems, particularly for the Cowal economy. The lure of higher wages quickly prompted many locals to turn their backs on their employers and make a beeline for the yard. In 1975, various businesses in Dunoon reported difficulties in recruiting staff while residents found it increasingly difficult to find tradesmen, like joiners, builders and electricians.

The Sunday Post of February 23, 1975, highlighted the crisis, reporting that since the project was launched the previous year, it had been 'almost impossible' to get joiners, plumbers, electricians, waitresses, and hotel staff in Dunoon.

Local men and woman were leaving their work and taking employment at Ardyne; their weekly wages shot up from £25 to as much as £150. For the first time in the history of the locality employers were complaining that local labour was scarce and that men and women who had been loyal employees over the years were leaving to follow the big money.

So difficult had it become to recruit staff that the Dunmore Hotel, amongst others, had been forced to convert to self-catering flats as they just could not find staff. One of their best waitresses had moved to the yard canteen where she was earning £60 a week.

Two greenkeepers from the town golf course had left to find new jobs at the yard while Wilson's Garage, on the Promenade, had lost 16 men, including mechanics and storemen. Bus drivers opted to apply for lorry and bus driving jobs at the yard, resulting in some local services being cut.

The newspaper quoted the local labour exchange which confirmed 200 local people had left their jobs in the town for the yard where the average pay was £100 a week. Even teaboys, it was said, have 'bulging' wage packets at the end of the week.

The Glasgow Herald highlighted the plight of Harry Graham, managing director of Cowal Motor Services, the sole public bus operator based in Dunoon. He needed nine drivers to cover all of his routes, but was down to just three. He was forced to cancel some of his bus routes and the services that did survive were reliant on garage mechanics, touring drivers and part-timers. He had also lost nine of his mechanics at his other business, West End Garage.

Local Provost Jack Thomson noted that McAlpine's had already bought a hotel in Dunoon for their workers and many others were being converted into flats, reducing the number of beds available to tourists.

One Dunoon man added: 'I know a lad who gets around £60 a week at McAlpine's for setting tables in the canteen. All he does is put out forks and knives as the men come in from their shifts and here I am with a miserable weekly wage of £28 for labouring.'

There were also claims that the yard led to the collapse of the Rothesay fishing fleet on the neighbouring Isle of Bute, luring away fishing boat crews with the promise of better wages.

Those in the local communities who had originally called on McAlpine to give priority to the local labour force were now furiously back-tracking and urging the company to only recruit workers from out with the area.

A study published in November 1974 indicated that 10% of the Ardyne workforce came from Dunoon, 1.4% from the rest of the Cowal peninsula and 5.3% from the neighbouring Isle of Bute. Almost a third – 30.7% - was drawn from Glasgow with an additional 20% coming from communities along the River Clyde like Gourock, Dumbarton and Renfrew.

There was also concern about the impact the yard was having on Dunoon's reputation as a holiday resort. Yard workers were moving into the hotels and guest houses and visitors were complaining that the navvies were sharing their holiday accommodation.

In addition to the 300 or so workers resident at the yard camp, a further 200, some married, lived in the Cowal community. McAlpine bought up property – hotels, flats and houses – in Dunoon to house its workers. Around 800 arrived daily on chartered ferries while 250 travelled to the site on scheduled ferries. Around 60 American technicians also worked for short periods in the yard.

In 1975, McAlpine secured the contract to widen and upgrade the road from Dunoon to Ardyne Point, the A815. The once twisty minor road was realigned, removing notorious bends, and pavements for pedestrians were added. During work at the yard, it was busy with lorries, green McAlpine vans, and buses transporting workers. However, in general, the improved route was well received by locals who had for many years been pressing the local council to do something about it.

Ardyne Point was no longer an outlying rural area where a few farmers lived and worked by the shores; it was now a vast industrial centre with national and international scope, home to an increasingly diverse and international labour force serving an international market for giant concrete structures that dwarfed the settlements and the hills of Cowal. Many locals felt a degree of alienation; they were no longer in control of their community but were powerless victims of decisions made far beyond their boundaries where money came first.

2

While the communities of Cowal grappled to get to grips with the new industrial hub in their midst, McAlpine's got down to the business of building oil platforms. Work on site commenced on February 4, 1974, with the shifting of spoil heaps, followed by the construction of the first basin. Six scrapers and various bulldozers and diggers were busy excavating the hole while steel for piling within the basin and the nearby wharf was on site ready to be used.

Construction had also begun on the concrete batching plant, located on flat ground to the north of the basins, while concrete aggregates were being stockpiled at Ayr Harbour ahead of transport by sea to the Ardyne wharf, as yet incomplete. An auxiliary concrete batcher was pressed into service while construction was underway on joiners' and fitters' shops.

Planning approval was expected for the camp accommodation, due to a change in location, although work was underway on the canteen and company offices and commissioning of electricity and telephone lines and a water supply, fed from the Ardyne Burn via tanks at the top of the site.

General site preparation was underway for the construction of both the Elf and the Shell/Esso platforms, and, at that time, 346 people were working at Ardyne. Of this, 273 were employed by McAlpine and 73 by various subcontractors.

The following month, good progress was being made on casting the skirt sections of *Frigg TP1*. While the site wharf remained incomplete, 1150 tonnes of aggregates, 705 tonnes of sand and 250 tonnes of cement, along with 1350 tonnes of steel reinforcing bars, were successfully delivered to enable work on the base to begin.

Much of the whinstone aggregate came from Hillhouse Quarries, near Irvine. McAlpine Sea Tank manufactured C50 concrete for the platforms. It is a high-performance concrete with a compressive strength of 50 newtons per square millimetre after 28 days of curing. It is commonly used for industrial structures operating in harsh environments where high levels of abrasion are present.

In April 1974, the company confirmed that construction of the first dry dock was complete and work on building the first base slab within it was now underway. The erection of the main concrete batcher for the Shell/Esso platform was also complete and work began on the base of *Brent Charlie* in what was now known as the Shell Basin, the more northerly of the two dry docks.

While *Brent Charlie* (Sea Mac II) was similar in design to *Frigg TP1* (Sea Mac I), it was larger and more complex. *Frigg TP1* had a base of 25 44-metre-high cells, measuring 72-metres long on each side. *Brent Charle's* square base measured 100 metres on all sides and consisted of 36 reinforced concrete cells, each 57 metres tall. It also had four 107-metre-tall legs rather than the two on the Elf unit.

Progress was also made on office accommodation and the accommodation camp. However, the good news was tempered by the fact that 47 joiners downed tools on an unofficial strike on April 18, effectively halting progress. They were vital to the project as they were involved in the construction of the vast wooden formers into which steel frames were set and the concrete was poured.

The joiners' strike continued into May resulting in limited progress on the platform and the temporary laying off of 41 labourers and 31 steel fixers. However, work did continue on the site infrastructure and the construction of the labour camp, the ground flattened ahead of the erection of Terrapin International modular buildings, temporary prefabricated structures. Aggregates and cement were now being delivered to the wharf in increasing amounts with healthy stockpiles growing on the site. The workforce had, however, dipped to 231, due to the strike, layoffs and a reduction in subcontractors.

June brought better news for the yard. McAlpine's reported that tests for the tow out were complete, and the striking joiners returned to work on June 11. Thereafter, with precasting of the skirts complete, construction of the *Frigg TP1* base got underway quickly and progressed well following the successful pouring of the base slab. The company was also now installing tower cranes for use in construction of the caissons while the workforce was more buoyant with 386 people on the Ardyne books.

By October 1974, the workforce had risen to 932 – 855 directly employed by McAlpine – and, with four tower cranes and concrete pouring pumps and booms operational within the dry dock now referred to as the Elf Basin, construction on the base of *Frigg TP1* was progressing well, growing to a height of three metres. Camp accommodation was also well in hand with 134 men in residence. Cement, sand, and aggregate continued to arrive by sea daily.

There were also regular deliveries of component parts that would be installed within the platform. These included pipework and mechanical and electrical parts that were vital to the operation of the completed platform and arrived at Ardyne, usually by boat, from factories around the country.

Slipform work – the pouring of concrete to form the metre-thick caisson walls – began on the nightshift of October 22/23 but ceased on the morning of October 25 when the steel fixers and scaffolders called an unofficial strike. They were followed three days later by electricians, plumbers, pipefitters and welders.

While cement, sand, and aggregate continued to arrive by sea, road deliveries to the yard were interrupted by striking workers who picketed the gates. Responding to the strike, which arose over bonus earnings, general working conditions, and what was described by a shop steward as a 'backlog of grievances', yard bosses sent telegrams to about 180 men telling them that if they did not turn up for work on Monday it would be assumed they had left the job.

After a two-hour meeting in Glasgow, the men, all members of the Transport and General Workers Union, criticised the 'Victorian attitude' of the management. Also at the meeting were 200 other strikers – scaffolders and pipefitters – who walked out in sympathy, and electricians who wanted their union recognised.

The telegrams prompted a gradual return to work and, by the end of November, 489 people were working in the yard with 163 employed on the Frigg platform. Despite the company's threat to sack steel fixers and scaffolders, industrial action by electricians, plumbers, pipefitters and welders continued through December 1974, further delaying progress. Slipform work was unable to resume, and the strike also impacted other projects in the yard, including progress on the accommodation and canteen.

The base of *Frigg TP1* taking shape in the dry dock in November 1974 – McAlpine Sea Tank

Dominated by tower cranes, the base of *Frigg TP1* takes shape in the dry dock in November 1974 – McAlpine Sea Tank

An aerial view of the yard in September 1974 showing the bases of *Brent Charlie* (left) and *Frigg TP1* in the dry docks – McAlpine Sea Tank

Attempted Heist on Payroll Van

There was some drama out with the yard towards the end of 1975, involving the Ardyne Point payroll van. Police received an anonymous telephone call informing them that armed Protestant extremists were planning to ambush it and steal the workers' wages, amounting to over £18,300.

The warning was taken seriously and the van was given a police escort from Glasgow Airport to Ardyne Point while detectives scoured Dunoon for the suspects, named as two local men, one of them Belfast-born with links to the Ulster Volunteer Force (UVF). They spotted the pair in a car and, as they followed, the vehicle stopped by the side of a loch. One of the men got out and threw a package into the water. This was retrieved and found to contain the barrel of a shotgun and two gun butts.

The two men were subsequently stopped and searched and one of them was found to have a note in his pocket on which was written a description of the payroll van and its registration number. Both were arrested and appeared at Glasgow High Court charged with conspiring to further the aims of the Ulster Volunteer Force (UVF) by obtaining firearms, ammunition and money and conspiring with each other to rob the payroll van of £18,368.

After a trial, they were convicted and, on March 19, 1976, the men were jailed for seven years each. They were both found guilty of conspiring to attack and rob the van at Innellan. They were also found guilty of possessing two sawn-off shotguns, another shotgun and ammunition with intent to endanger life.

Thanks to the anonymous tip-off and swift action of the police, the payroll van arrived safely at the yard and the workers received their wages.

The base of *Frigg TP1* in the flooded dry dock in February 1975 ahead of float-out – McAlpine Sea Tank

An aerial view of *Frigg TP1* in the flooded dry dock in February 1975 ahead of float-out – McAlpine Sea Tank

The strike of November and December 1974 was finally resolved on January 17, 1975, when the electricians, plumbers, pipefitters and welders returned to work and slip forming the base of the Elf platform restarted two days later with progress being reported as good. During February the height of the caissons increased and work began on preparing for its float-out from the dry dock, a significant step forward in the project which was gradually falling behind schedule due to the regular strikes; February was no exception and saw three separate disputes.

On February 10, members of the Amalgamated Union of Engineering Workers (AUEW) – mainly crane operators and fitters – began working a 40-hour week in a bid to gain union recognition. Four days later they downed tools completely following the sacking of one of their shop stewards. The steward was reinstated on February 18 and the men returned to working a 40-hour week. Two days after that, following a meeting between management and the men, they returned to normal working.

On February 11, lorry drivers stopped working following the sacking of one of their colleagues. They remained on strike for three days before the matter was resolved. The day after the drivers returned to work, canteen staff walked out in a dispute over pay. They returned to work on February 19.

On a more positive note, four of the eight men's dormitory blocks were finished complete, as was accommodation for office staff and executives, and a small church building and there was good progress on the canteen extension which was due to open the following month.

Meanwhile, in the Elf Basin, significant progress had been made on the construction and fitting out of the platform base. On the night of February 8/9, the dry dock was finally flooded, and water was pumped into the caissons to ballast it so it did not float when the seawall was removed. Dredging work to remove the seawall started days later and, on March 12, the platform base was successfully refloated and towed out of the Elf Basin to its new position, 150-metres offshore, where it was moored to blocks on the seabed ahead of construction work continuing. Equipment barges and pontoons were moored alongside the platform and a pontoon bridge installed to link it to the shoreline and enable workers to access it. This was fitted with pipelines to allow concrete to be pumped out.

Slip forming began on the evening of April 8 and by midnight on April 20, the caisson walls achieved a height of 13.5 metres and bosses reported that the work was progressing satisfactorily.

The base of *Frigg TP1* moored in Loch Striven after a successful float-out – McAlpine Sea Tank

Despite being around five weeks behind schedule due to strikes, the float out milestone was celebrated, both at the yard and in the Press. On March 13, *The Scotsman* reported that it was the first of four concrete platforms under construction in the UK to be floated out.

'The base caisson, named Sea Mac I, and comprising 17,500 tonnes of concrete, was towed from its flooded basin by five tugs and coaxed into Loch Striven,' the article continue. 'There the structure will be moored for the next six or seven months while slip forming of the remaining 160,000 tonnes of concrete in the base and two columns takes place.'

The report also revealed that Ardyne Point, now described as the 'world's largest platform yard', was tendering for another contract, in competition with the Howard-Doris yard on Loch Kishorn and the government-funded facilities at Portavadie and Hunterston.

By the end of April 1975 McAlpine was employing 548 people at the yard with a further 228 workers deployed to the Elf rig. There were also 254 people employed by subcontractors on the site. Progress was made on the prefabricated camp accommodation, now largely complete and partly occupied, and the small church included in the project held its first service on April 20.

While work continued on the Elf platform in Loch Striven, photographs taken at the time indicate that within the Shell Basin, equally good progress was being made on the base of *Brent Charlie*.

In May, McAlpine reported that slip forming of the caisson walls of the Elf platform was complete and the roof shuttering, fabricated within the yard, was being lifted into place by crane barge with eight of the 12 complete.

McAlpine had originally contracted to deliver the platform to Elf Norge by May 15, 1975, but, as the deadline passed, it was clear that platform construction was at least two months behind schedule. There were also delays to its topside, or module support frame, being constructed at the Mardyck yard in the French port of Dunkerque and mating the two units was postponed.

In a bid to speed up work on the Elf platform, management drafted in Neptun Salvage's *Hebe 2*, at the time Europe's largest barge-mounted crane with an 800-tonne lifting capacity. It supplemented the efforts of the tower cranes mounted on the platform.

The base of *Frigg TP1* progressing in Loch Striven in July 1975 - McAlpine Sea Tank

Meanwhile, in the Shell Basin, *Brent Charlie* was nearing its float-out. By mid-May the basin had been flooded and the dock gate removed ready for it to emerge into Loch Striven. The following month it was towed out of the basin into Loch Striven and moored on blocks 150-metres offshore in a position just north of *Frigg TP1*. Again, it was linked to the yard by a pontoon.

Over on the Elf platform, work was progressing 'satisfactorily' with the focus on strengthening the base slab and installing the caisson cell roofs before work began on the two leg towers on July 9. At this stage, there were 243 men working on the platform with a further 457 employed in the yard, most working on the Shell/Esso platform.

The base of *Frigg TP1* from the pontoon bridge installed to link it to the shoreline – McAlpine Sea Tank

Work progressed through the summer with the intention of towing the completed platform out to a site in Loch Fyne in November 1975. On November 19, 1975, *The Scotsman* reported that the platform was 'almost complete' and was only lacked its deck and modules.

Delays led to this being pushed back to March 1976. As the project neared completion, 300 men working at the yard for subcontractors Wimpey went on strike, demanding severance pay and an extra allowance for working at the remote site, forcing Elf to threaten to transfer the final modification work abroad.

The base of *Frigg TP1* nearing completion, thanks to the help of Neptun Salvage's *Hebe 2* barge crane – John Scott

The Scotsman article also hinted at a less than optimistic future for the Ardyne Point yard. While work progressed in Loch Striven on the *Brent Charlie* and *Cormorant Alpha* (Sea Mac III) platforms, both behind schedule but due for completion in 1977, the two dry docks remained empty due to an 'order famine'.

An aerial view of *Frigg TP1* nearing completion – McAlpine Sea Tank

Despite the strike, the completed 166,000 tonne *Frigg TP1* finally departed Loch Striven on March 22, 1976, and it was towed south through the Firth of Clyde, into the deeper waters of Loch Fyne, where it was anchored off Barmore Island, just north of Tarbert, and lowered to a depth of 120 metres. Ironically, it now sat within view of the Portavadie platform yard, which had yet to receive an order.

Tugs preparing to tow *Frigg TP1* from Loch Striven to Loch Fyne, with the *Brent Charlie* base visible to the left – McAlpine Sea Tank

The steel module support frame and the topside modules towed on barges to Loch Fyne from France were successfully attached to the tops of the two legs by a pair of mighty crane barges and the finished platform was raised in the water ahead of its long journey to the Frigg gas field.

While the two sections of the platform were successfully mated, the eight-week operation was not without incident. The *Aberdeen Evening Express* of May 13, 1976, reported that a 24-year-old diver died while working on the platform. Nicholas Hubert, who was employed by North Sea Diving Services on the barge *PT One Elfa Norge*, was looking for a faulty transponder on the bottom of the platform, at a depth of around 60 metres. After an uneventful dive, he was returning to the surface when he died. The cause of death was reported as AGE (Arterial Gas Embolism).

Frigg TP1 with its topside successfully attached in Loch Fyne – Elf/ Norwegian Petroleum Museum

Towed by a fleet of five tugs at speeds of less than 5mph, the platform left Loch Fyne, journeyed up the west coast of Scotland and on northwards to the Shetland Islands before travelling east to the Frigg field. The tow was largely uneventful and completed ahead of schedule.

On June 5, 1976, the platform was lowered into position in 104 metres of water, coming to rest on the seabed where it was held in place by gravity and some seawater ballasting. Once installed, it was connected to its two neighbouring platforms by gangways and production modules were hoisted aboard.

Back at Ardyne Point, with one contract complete, construction of Shell/Esso's *Brent Charlie* and *Cormorant Alpha* platforms continued apace in Loch Striven. Photographs indicate that work on the larger Cormorant Alpha, moored to the south of the dry docks, was ahead of *Brent Charlie*, probably due to McAlpine's decision to move from concrete pouring to the assembly of precast sections. *The Scotsman* newspaper of July 22,

1975, reported that the company had drafted in more men to increase productivity. It claimed the workforce at Ardyne Point now numbered some 3000.

Rather than complete the platforms in Loch Fyne, Shell/Esso insisted that the bases be towed to Norway for mating with their topsides. This was done in a bid to save costs and speed up installation.

The more complex base of *Cormorant Alpha* under construction in the dry dock – McAlpine Sea Tank

On June 16, 1977, *The Scotsman* reported that one of the platforms was due to be towed away that month with the other following in July, leaving behind a bleak future for the 600 or so people still employed at the yard.

McAlpine Sea Tank and operators Shell/Esso were also left counting the cost. While the original contracts predicted that *Brent*

Charlie would cost £24 million and *Cormorant Alpha* £33 million, the final costs of the platforms amounted to £75 million and £115 million respectively. This did not include costs associated with the delays to installation and lost oil revenue but did include a contribution to McAlpine's outlay in preparing the land at Ardyne Point. Shell/Esso paid McAlpine monthly, based on progress and, in the end, the firm received £190 million for the two Shell/Esso platforms.

Despite delays caused by both industrial action and design changes, Shell/Esso believed many of the problems of the first two years were a phase that passed and described the productivity and progress achieved in the last 18 months of the work programme at Ardyne as 'most impressive'. Although it was obviously impossible to recover the time lost in the early stages, the operator was reportedly 'most gratified' by the final progress achieved. The contract work at Ardyne was deemed a success only troubled by factors beyond control of both client and contractor.

Brent Charlie (left) and *Cormorant Alpha* under construction at Ardyne Point – Sir Robert McAlpine & Sons Ltd

The completed *Frigg TP1* platform – Elf/Norwegian Petroleum Museum

3

The Ardyne Point yard was established at the south-western end of the most easterly of the arms of the Cowal peninsula. It ultimately occupied around 100 acres of land bordering Loch Striven and extended for a mile along the shoreline, bounded to the east by farmland and the Ardyne Burn, beyond which the land sloped up to heavily forested hills.

While McAlpine Sea Tank initially occupied only 40 acres of the site, they swiftly extended it north, partly to prevent a competitor gaining a foothold on the Loch Striven shoreline and partly to allow the company to construct up to six platforms at any one time. The land had previously been used for the grazing of some 450 sheep and provided a shoreline habitat for wildlife.

Accessed by a roadway that branched off the minor road at a point near Toward Quay, a little over a mile from the southern end of the A815, the main route south from Dunoon, the yard was entered beyond a bridge spanning the tidal mouth of the Ardyne Burn. This was upgraded to a steel span to cope with the weight of traffic and a second parallel access road was later constructed to the north of this, again linking with the minor Glenstriven Road.

Entering the yard from the south, the two dry docks sit to the left. The more southerly one was referred to as the Elf Basin while its slightly larger neighbour was the Shell Basin. One concrete batcher plant, complete with cement silos and stockpiles of aggregate, sand and cement, was established adjacent to the Elf Basin and a second concrete batcher plant was located on the north side of the Shell Basin. Both were linked to their respective basins by pipes and pumps located on the side banks of the basins. Concrete ramps descended into the basins to provide access for men and machinery and floodlighting was installed to allow work in the basins to continue around the clock. McAlpine's men were employed on 12-hour shifts due to the nature of the work. Slip forming often continued for 24 hours a day over periods of many days, sometimes weeks.

The sign at the entrance to the yard

The remainder of the land around the basins was occupied by what can only be described as a 'shanty town' of temporary buildings. With the yard only expected to have an operational life of 10 to 15 years, no permanent structures were built, other than the electricity substation. Instead, blocks of portable cabins provided office space while corrugated iron sheds housed heated workshops and stores, and a plethora of smaller wooden sheds dotted in between served as shelters and break rooms for the workers. Car parks and open storage areas for steel and component parts filled most of the empty spaces. The workshops and portable cabins were grounded on concrete foundations and some concrete walls were erected to keep the stockpiles in order.

Individual offices were provided for McAlpine, Sea Tank, Elf and Shell staff working on the site, served by 50 telephone lines installed by the General Post Office while a large canteen was erected opposite the offices. This opened in March 1975.

An aerial view of the yard – McAlpine Sea Tank

Mains electricity was routed into a small substation located behind the Shell Basin, water was diverted from the Ardyne Burn, a water treatment and sewage plant was constructed, and a network of concrete roads was laid down to connect the various parts of the yard.

The yard had its own full time fire service; there were at least two fire appliances, and a small unit of full-time station staff was supplemented by workers from the yard, who attended regular training courses. There was also a private ambulance and medical centre (the nearest hospital was in Dunoon).

A wharf to receive deliveries of aggregate, sand and cement by sea was constructed on the other side of a low headland to the north of the Shell Basin while the road proceeded north, passing the camp accommodation, a sprawling township of rows of green Terrapin modular buildings occupying levelled ground to the north of the Shell Basin. Mounted on concrete foundations and served by its own network of roads, the camp was built in three phases. By November 1974, the first two phases were complete, and 220 men were living in the camp. This would later total over 300. The Terrapin International buildings were manufactured at the company's site in Glenrothes, Fife, before being transported west to Ardyne Point.

The camp included a small wooden church which, with the agreement of the local Church of Scotland minister, was intended to be for interdenominational use. In reality, the facility was only really used by Catholics and was furnished with an altar, confessional and various statues. Well-attended Masses were held every Sunday at 6pm by a local priest and collections benefited both the church and the local community. So well attended were these masses that the wee church was just not big enough and some of the men, oilskins dripping with wet cement, had to stand outside. Many of the men who lived in the camp were navvies of Irish descent – occasionally referred to as McAlpine's Fusiliers – who formed the core of the company's itinerant workforce, moving from one big contract to the next. While the local Church of Scotland minister did attempt to connect with those of Presbyterian faith, due to lack of numbers, this ended unsuccessfully.

Beyond the accommodation camp, a single road continued north to a third basin carved out in 1975 in the northern corner of the yard. This was smaller than the two platform basins and was not at any point used as a dry dock to construct a platform. It served primarily as a harbour and wharf for ferries and delivery boats, enjoying a more sheltered position from the prevailing winds and tides.

Based on timelines detailed in monthly reports compiled by McAlpine Sea Tank for Elf, the yard was by no means complete or indeed ready for work to start on the first concrete platform, *Frigg FP1*. Instead, it appears to have grown organically with it, meeting the needs of the platform and adapting as it progressed. Digging the great basins in which the platforms took their early shape and mounding up sufficient quantities of gravel, sand and cement to produce the vast amount of concrete needed clearly took priority over accommodating the workers, or even the office staff, with expanding canteen facilities, utilities, and the prefabricated digs chasing the tail of the mighty leviathans emerging from the first and then second shoreline basin.

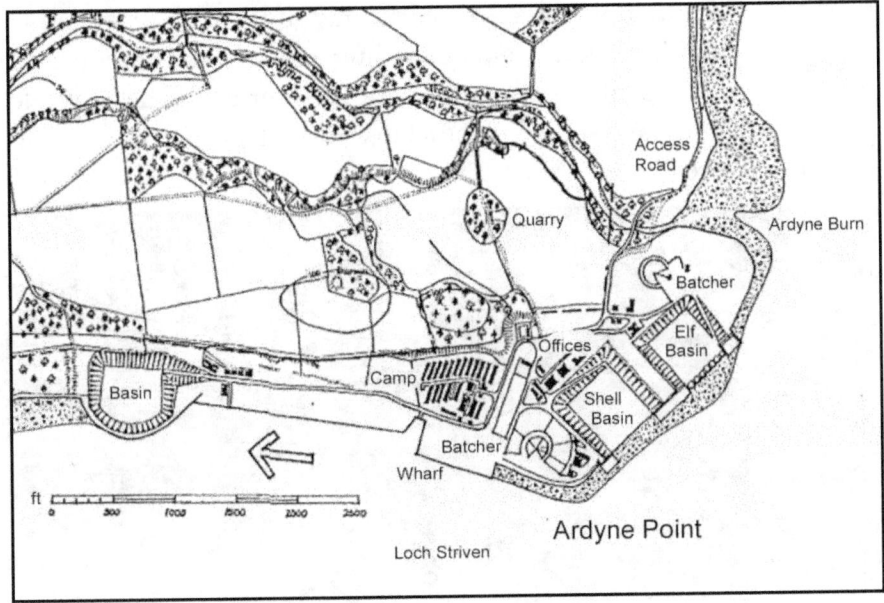

A map showing the layout of the yard

The reports, archived by the Norwegian Petroleum Museum, also demonstrate the fluctuating nature of the labour force, from the first 78 people employed in the yard when work commenced in February 1974, to an early peak of around 1000 the following year. The number of workers was constantly fluctuating, in part due to regular strikes, with McAlpine Sea Tank, particularly in the early days, preferring to simply sack striking workers and recruit new ones rather than negotiate with unions. This American-influenced form of industrial relations eased as the firm, under pressure from the big oil companies, raced to make up lost time on its delayed projects. However, in later years it was reported that the strikes had less to do with the management and more to do with an escalating conflict between two unions, out with the control of McAlpine Sea Tank.

Figures indicate that of these 1000 or so workers, around 300, mainly itinerant navvies, were living within the camp accommodation. A further 200, mainly support staff working in the offices and canteen, were drawn from the Cowal community while the remainder travelled each day by ferry. Over time, McAlpine acquired hotels and boarding houses in Dunoon and the local area to provide accommodation closer to the base, while some managers and senior technicians bought property, pushing up house prices.

The navvy camp – McAlpine Sea Tank

Those arriving at Ardyne by sea were split between workers from Glasgow and the Clyde who used the scheduled ferries from Gourock to Dunoon. However, McAlpine Sea Tank also chartered their own sailings, one contracted to Caledonian MacBrayne, which, from March to October 1974, sailed daily from Wemyss Bay to a pier at Innellan, midway between Dunoon and the yard, bringing in workers from Inverclyde and Ayrshire. After October 1974, the pier at Innellan was abandoned and services were routed direct to the wharf at Ardyne.

Passenger facilities aboard Caledonian MacBrayne's *MV Keppel*, an ex-British Rail vessel, were described as 'spartan' while the boat was slow but reliable, making the crossing in half an hour. She had a passenger capacity of 340 and made four sailings a day to and from Ardyne, timed to coincide with the beginning and end of shifts. From time to time, other Caledonian MacBrayne vessels operated the run, including *MV Bute* and *MV Cowal* while *MV Glen Sannox* took over the run during peak periods of work at the yard, due to her larger passenger capacity and remained in service on the route for two years.

MV Glen Sannox passing the *Cormorant Alpha* base in 1976

McAlpine Sea Tank also operated its own passenger ferry, using *Queen of Scots*, which sailed from Rothesay, on the neighbouring Isle of Bute, to the yard. The boat, which could accommodate 470 passengers, was acquired by McAlpine in 1973 and sold in June 1977.

McAlpine Sea Tank also contracted the services of Western Ferries, a company that pioneered roll-on roll-off ferries in the Firth of Clyde, to transport freight to Ardyne Point. Using *Sound of Islay*, the company commenced a regular service from McInroy's Point, Gourock, to Ardyne on July 30, 1974. A number of return trips were made each day with cement and other cargo, often squeezed in between the scheduled Gourock to Hunter's Quay ferry service. Oil-related contracts generated around 40% of Western Ferries profits at this time.

To provide a quicker means of transport to Ardyne Point for managers and important visitors, McAlpine Sea Tank initially chartered helicopters from a company based at Glasgow Airport. However, in 1974, Sir Robert McAlpine & Sons Ltd, which had its Scottish headquarters at the airport, established its own subsidiary, McAlpine Helicopters, operating a Gazelle (G-BBHW). The helicopter was initially based at Inverkip, Greenock, where McAlpine was constructing a power station, but was later transferred to Glasgow Airport. In addition to ferrying staff and guests to the yard, the Gazelle made frequent trips to Ardyne Point to undertake aerial photography of the platforms under construction. The photographs were appended to monthly update reports sent to Elf and Shell/Esso.

The helicopter was made available for general charters when not flying to and from Ardyne Point and, in 2007, McAlpine Helicopters was acquired by Airbus and was renamed Airbus Helicopters UK in 2014.

The Ardyne Point yard was off-limits to local people, other than those employed there, although occasionally opened its gates to pre-arranged Press calls and visits by politicians and oil industry leaders. Management often nipped in and out by helicopter and there was little contact with the people of Cowal. However, in March 1975, following the successful float out of the *Frigg TP1* platform, McAlpine Sea Tank took steps to involve and inform the local community, commissioning Inland & Waterside Planners to publish a booklet entitled *Ardyne Tomorrow* in which a pledge was made to restore the site once construction work was complete. The report was the first published after-use plan for a North Sea oil related site. It also discussed possible future uses for the site and was designed to allay concerns expressed locally over the environment and employment at the site.

Ardyne Tomorrow suggested that the yard could become an adventure and education complex complete with a sail training school and yachting marina, or a fish farm with marine laboratory. Both ideas were mooted as being economically more practical than filling in the basins for a total return to 'the sheep and seagulls'. Inland and Waterside Planners proposed making use of the costly civil engineering already undertaken and turning it to the advantage of the environment and the report's authors stated a preference for a mix of activities and social and commercial enterprises.

An artist's impression of a marina at Ardyne Point, published in *Ardyne Tomorrow*

The forward stated: 'Sir Robert McAlpine & Sons are pledged to the restoration of their oil platform construction site at Ardyne at the conclusion of their leases and planning permissions.'

The document warned that, due to the fast-moving nature of the oil industry and platform technology, Ardyne's place in the North Sea oil story would last 'perhaps 10 years' but suggested, in future, Ardyne Point could serve as a as day-to-day service base, hinting that it would not be completely abandoned.

Initial landscaping work had already begun to 'soften' the site, with an artificial hill created from excavated spoil now being planted with trees. The hill overlooked the platform site and reduced the impact of high-rise construction work and equipment on the skyline.

The booklet was officially launched at a ceremony where the Marquis of Bute planted 35 trees on the hillside and, while clearly a public relations exercise, did prompt plenty of debate in the Cowal community with many looking forward to the creation of a new marina, one of six options presented. The yard, however, still had a couple of years left in it and there was always the possibility that McAlpine Sea Tank might secure further platforms...

Frigg TP1 with the yard behind – McAlpine Sea Tank

4

With the two platforms under construction at Ardyne Point due to depart in the summer of 1977, prospects for the yard, in common with others, looked bleak. Both the *Brent Charlie* and *Cormorant Alpha* platforms were a year behind schedule, prompting a heated outburst from Shell's chairman, Sir Frank McFadzean, directed not at McAlpine Sea Tank but at the government. He argued that the decision to select the Clyde area for platform construction was 'purely political', adding that Ardyne Point was 'physically unsuitable' and had become an 'albatross' around the necks of McAlpine and Sea Tank.

His opinion contrasted with views expressed during the rush to establish yards, when Ardyne Point was viewed by many as offering perhaps the best site in Europe for concrete platform construction on a major scale. However, it was clear that the oil and gas operators were not beating a path to Scotland's door for concrete platforms. Aside from the three commissioned at Ardyne Point, only one other was built in Scotland, the Ninian Central, constructed at Loch Kishorn and completed in 1978.

An order famine was identified in 1975 with both speculative government-based yards at Portavadie and Hunterston failing to secure any work while Norway, by contrast, continued to prosper. On February 4, 1976, *The Scotsman* reported that the Ardyne Point yard could close the following year unless it won more orders. Management had informed Argyll District Council that it could cease operations in Spring 1977 and, early in 1975, began a programme of layoffs to reduce the workforce, a move that prompted more sporadic strike action. By the end of the year, a quarter of the Ardyne Point workforce had been dismissed.

Cormorant Alpha base under construction at the yard – Hugh Gillies/British Geological Survey

The dire warning came as McAlpine's prepared to float the base of *Cormorant Alpha* out of dry dock. The firm claimed that once this was done its dry docks would be empty and it would need three new platform orders to secure the future of its workforce. Some £20 million had been invested in the site with a view to constructing 15 or more platforms by 1985 and the company had demonstrated an efficient platform construction process, hindered only by industrial disputes which were not uncommon in Britain in the 1970s.

The local council planning director Michael Oliver described the future as 'cloudy', but the ever-optimistic government-run Offshore Supplies Office in Glasgow predicted that the industry would order between four and six platforms in 1976, another seven in 1977 and a further 17 from 1978-80, adding that McAlpine Sea Tank was in an 'excellent position' to bid for these.

Cormorant Alpha in Loch Striven in February 1977 – British Geological Survey

Early in July 1977, the last of the three platforms completed at Ardyne Point, the 270,000 tonne *Brent Charlie*, was towed out of Loch Striven by a fleet of six tugs, on the start of a 900-mile sea journey to Stord, Norway, where the deck structures and modules would be mounted atop its four towering concrete legs ahead of installation in the North Sea. The fleet of tugs was returning to Scotland after a successful 12-day journey delivering *Cormorant Alpha* to Stord on July 3 for mating with her topside.

Despite being the second platform to leave the dry dock, *Brent Charlie's* completion was delayed by 20 months due to some of the most major design changes imposed on any platform builder, along with a plethora of strikes.

As it left Loch Striven, management at the yard were quick to dismiss suggestions that concrete platforms had become a 'technological dodo', pledging their faith in the concept and their ability to win more orders.

In an article in the *Aberdeen Press & Journal* of July 9, 1977, an unnamed spokesman for the yard is quoted as saying: 'Despite recent ill-informed comment, the concrete gravity structure as exemplified by the three built at Ardyne Point is not a technological dodo. Its role as a viable production unit in the North Sea and elsewhere is being actively studied even now by some of the largest companies in the world. Every effort is being made to introduce fresh work to Ardyne Point, a design and construction engineering installation unique in the world with a proven track record of technological achievement.'

Brent Charlie nearing completion – McAlpine Sea Tank

This probably came as little consolation to the hundreds of workers now being laid off at the yard which had failed to secure any more work for them. While many of McAlpine's Fusiliers moved on to other contracts around the country – a significant number chasing the oil industry to Aberdeen and the yards of the north-east and Highlands – those facing the bleakest futures were the dozens of local men and women who had turned their backs on employers in the Cowal community in favour of the larger wages on offer at Ardyne Point; they now faced the difficult task of returning home cap in hand and many opted to leave Cowal for good.

The company statement was swiftly contradicted by reports published later that year which indicated there was no future for concrete platform construction in Scotland. On October 25, 1977, *The Scotsman* reported that the Department of Energy's earlier optimism had now turned to pessimism and, with no orders in sight, it was moving towards scrapping its investment in yards at Portavadie and Hunterston, intending to close both mothballed sites the following year.

McAlpine Sea Tank pledged to retain the Ardyne Point yard until at least the end of 1978 but it too was of the view that no more concrete platforms would be built in Scotland, based on the results of its own intensive marketing campaign.

With the prospect of securing no more oil platform work, the firm's designers and engineers turned their attentions to developing other maritime concrete-based construction projects, including floating harbours and hotels, processing plants, accommodation modules and enclosed seabed production facilities.

Initially the company, in partnership with an American offshore concrete engineering group, conducted a feasibility study for concrete barges to transport a new chemical plant from the UK to a customer in the Middle East. The order, if secured, would occupy one of the basins at Ardyne Point.

Marine Week, of November 5, 1976, reported that McAlpine Sea Tank had signed a licensing agreement to build a semi-submersible concrete barge/platform structure to the design of Trans-Energy International. The company planned to market the new structure for oil and gas production as well as for processing and storage of gas.

Cormorant Alpha ready to be towed out of Loch Striven – McAlpine Sea Tank

Their concrete-based range of barge-mounted plants was christened *MacPlat* and it was reported that the firm came close to securing an order for a deoxygenation plant for the Persian Gulf oil wells.

Marine Week, of February 18, 1977, reported that McAlpine was 'making a big effort to diversify with a new design of concrete barge designed to form the permanent base for a range of industrial and commercial projects.

'The concept involves using the basins at Ardyne Point to build the basic barges, which would then be floated out and fitted with chemical plants, desalination equipment, fully self-contained hotels and even a whole refinery.'

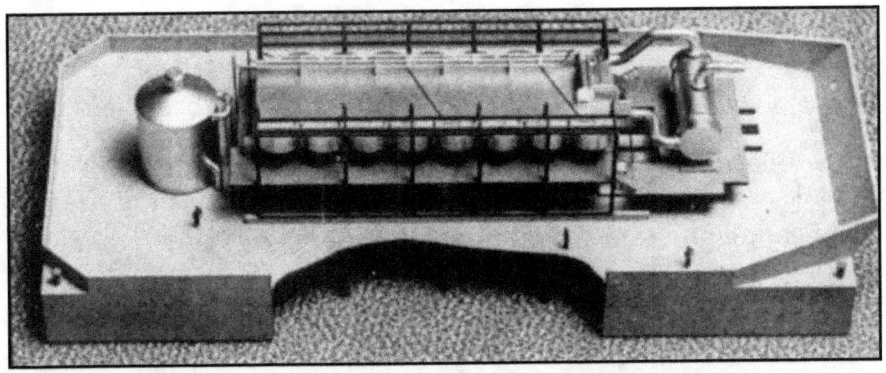

A model of a *MacPlat* barge with desalination equipment

After construction at Ardyne, the barges – which would range from 315ft by 118ft for a 520-room hotel complete with power plant, sewage treatment and water supply, to 164ft by 75ft for a desalination plant – would be towed to a location with prefabricating facilities for completion.

Ocean Industry magazine, of November 1976, reported that McAlpine Sea Tank, with future orders for the Ardyne Point yard in mind, had devised such concepts as the *Macplat* prestressed concrete platform, closely followed by the underwater *Subseamac* range of installations.

'McAlpine Sea Tank could use Ardyne Point to build the modules using techniques employed for gravity platforms,' the magazine continued. 'The base storage caisson is similar in proportion to those being used in gravity units. The base would be built to 15 metres and then floated out and completed inshore. The modules on top would be installed in deeper water. At the field site, 12 hours of good weather would be needed to ballast the unit to nominal positive buoyancy and then winch it to the seabed. Then the ballast load would be increased, and grouting could be carried out if desired.'

The *Subseamac* venture proposed by McAlpine would do away with conventional surface rigs and it envisaged placing a complete offshore oil field production system underwater. Christened *Subseamac One*, the towers of a traditional gravity platform were eliminated by placing deck equipment inside a series of concrete modules set directly on top of the base caisson.

Despite investing time and money in developing *Macplat* and *Subseamac*, which included commissioning a variety of academic, engineering and safety reports, the North Sea oil industry, among various potential customers, failed to bite and neither of these innovative projects brought any work to Ardyne Point.

Cormorant Alpha being towed out of Loch Striven at the start of its long voyage to Norway – McAlpine Sea Tank

Rather than close the site, McAlpine Sea Tank initially chose to mothball it, retaining 50 employees and spending £250,000 a year running it on a care and maintenance basis, preferring to view the tow out of *Brent Charlie* as the end of a chapter rather than the story.

Planning consent was regularly renewed into the 1990s while, as the 1970s progressed with no sign of any construction work, the company investigated alternative uses, including basing a fish farm in one of the dry dock basins. Other options included a marina, sports centre or holiday resort.

A family watch the departure of *Brent Charlie* from Loch Striven from a beach on the Isle of Bute – Bute Museum

5

After the departure of the third and final concrete platform from Ardyne Point, McAlpine retained the yard on a care and maintenance basis and, over the years, various proposals for the site were put forward. With plans coming and going, and questions being asked in the House of Commons, the issue of what would become of the yard was frequently referred to as a 'saga' by the Press.

McAlpine were, however, clearly not ready to let the yard go and, on August 2, 1978, successfully renewed its planning consent for the continued use of Ardyne Point for the construction of offshore oil production platforms and other floating concrete and steel structures for a further period of six years. However, the council demanded that work commence before December 31, 1979, or the permission would lapse.

The last platform to leave Loch Striven – *Brent Charlie* – with *Cormorant Alpha* in the background – McAlpine Sea Tank

In 1979 the company lodged another planning application with the local council for a fish farm adjacent to the most northern of the three basins. Permission was granted and the development proceeded.

It was clear that while McAlpine was keen to re-open the site, it was slowly running Ardyne Point down. Observers suggested the fish farm development effectively ended any hope the yard might win more North Sea orders and, on July 29, 1979, *The Sunday Post* reported that many of the hundreds of portable cabins, sheds, and huts set up on the site during the yard's heyday had now gone. It quoted a care-and-maintenance worker as saying: 'Every time McAlpine get a new contract they come here first for buildings. Ardyne's just a store for them.'

In the summer of 1979 the company awarded a contract to clear scrap from the site, another indication that there was no future for North Sea orders and it was preparing the land for alternative uses, and perhaps fulfilling its commitment to clean it up.

Among the men sent to remove the scrap, was former train robber Bruce Reynolds. The *Glasgow Evening Times* reported that the 48-year-old was seen heaving scrap aboard a boat at the yard.

Reynolds masterminded the 1963 Great Train Robbery. At the time it was Britain's largest robbery, netting over £2 million. After five years on the run, he was arrested and, admitting his part in the famous heist, he was sentenced to 25 years in prison. He was released early in 1978 and, as a friend of the director of the company that received the contract to move scrap from the site, was reportedly looking to earn some money after a successful tour promoting the paperback edition of his book about the robbery. Unlike his fellow workers he did not live on the site but stayed in the more comfortable surroundings of a hotel in Dunoon.

McAlpine continued to renew its planning consent for use of the yard for production of concrete structures and these applications were granted in January 1980, November 1987 and January 1997.

In early 1990, offshore experts suggested concrete oil production platforms may be ready to make a comeback in the UK, claiming that operator Amerada Hess favoured a concrete substructure for the new Scott field. Concrete platforms were re-emerging following Hamilton Brothers Petroleum's success with the *Ravenspurne North* platform which turned out to be cheaper to build and quicker to install than steel alternatives.

The Oil & Gas Journal reported that McAlpine Offshore, a subsidiary of Sir Robert McAlpine & Sons Ltd, and Doris Engineering, which had earlier merged with Sea Tank, had formed a joint venture to undertake complete design, construction, and installation for new concrete structures in the North Sea.

The McAlpine Doris consortium was reportedly likely to build the structures at Ardyne Point, stating that one advantage of concrete construction was that a facility does not take long to set up.

'We can mobilise Ardyne Point to be building there within two months,' marketing director Mike Banning-Lover is quoted as saying.

However, Amerada Hess eventually opted for two steel platforms and the venture did not result in any work for Ardyne Point.

In 1995 McAlpine was part of a consortium bidding to win the contract for a floating production facility for BP's Fionaven field, west of Shetland. The intention was to build a ship-shaped concrete production, storage and offloading platform at Ardyne Point. However, the contract did not go to the consortium, BP opting for a steel-hulled vessel.

Plans were also granted in May 1983 to use the site for the storage and shipping of timber and, in August 1986 permission was granted to Glenlight Shipping Limited for the formation of a timber storage and vessel loading area.

Another fish farm proposal by Murray Seafoods Limited was granted permission in August 1989 which, if it had gone ahead, would have seen the construction of a processing facility and offices.

One of the most controversial proposals to surface was to use the yard for the dismantling of decommissioned nuclear submarines under a Ministry of Defence initiative named Project ISOLUS (Interim Storage of Laid-up Submarines). In 2000, Sir Robert McAlpine Ltd was one of five companies to express an interest in the work. According to council papers, it submitted a proposal for both the dismantling of the submarines and the interim storage (up to 50 years) of the radioactive reactor compartments.

McAlpine's proposal to the MoD was to evaluate and consult upon the possible renovation and use of the disused construction docks at Ardyne Point to cut up decommissioned and de-fuelled nuclear submarines. The reactor compartments would be removed intact from the submarines and stored in purpose-built facilities on site. Later the reactor compartments might be cut up in additional purpose-built facilities to reduce their volume prior to long term storage in a national waste management facility.

Project ISOLUS included a public consultation process where local communities were invited to have their say and, in 2003, there was very vocal opposition to McAlpine's plans. The people of Cowal and Bute reacted strongly against the idea of using Ardyne Point, fearing that the submarine scrapyard might damage the area's tourist industry and impact upon its reputation for whisky, shellfish and salmon. An avalanche of letters of protest was sent and angry residents received cross-party support from politicians. The strength of the opposition prompted McAlpine to withdraw its interest in the project.

The company returned to the drawing board and, in 2006, submitted plans for a £100 million mixed use development comprising a hotel, marina, shops and housing. The project envisaged turning the dry docks into a 220-berth marina beside which there would be a 120-bed hotel, restaurant, shops and offices. Some 220 houses and apartments would be built on the site along with car parking and a ferry terminal. The project would involve the partial infill of the Elf Basin.

Argyll and Bute council granted planning permission and discussions continued over the next five or so years. However, in the end, the development did not proceed, the consent lapsed, and, in August 2013, it was reported that McAlpine ended its links with Ardyne Point, selling the land to an Edinburgh-based property developer, Ardyne Estates Ltd.

The new owners subsequently drew up a masterplan for the brownfield site, proposing a mixed-use development, starting with a new fish processing facility, associated infrastructure and a new road access crossing the field from the Glenstriven Road. The plan included areas for tourism, business, leisure, housing, marine, and aquaculture developments.

The remains of wharfs on the site – Thomas Nugent

CONCRETE GIANTS OF ARDYNE POINT

The remains of one of the dry docks – Thomas Nugent

Surviving floor and walls of one of the fitters' shops – Thomas Nugent

6

In the heady early days of the North Sea oil and gas rush, when efforts were being made to secure platform contracts and get production underway in the new fields as quicky as possible, little if any thought was given to what would happen to the platforms once their working lives were at an end.

Now, over 40 years on, the three platforms built at Ardyne Point are no longer in production and the thorny question of what to do with the thousands of tonnes of concrete has raised its head. Part of the problem is that the bases were all designed and installed before any requirement for removability of such structures was introduced in the North Sea. The equipment fitted to each to enable their installation only had a short lifespan, rendering it now largely obsolete, and, to date, no one has successfully refloated a concrete platform that has been sat on the seabed for four decades.

Frigg TP1 was the first to be decommissioned. Production on the Norwegian-UK gas field ceased in the autumn of 2004 and plans were drawn up and submitted for disposal of the platforms. All topsides, steel jackets and equipment were removed from the field and taken ashore for recycling or reuse.

However, what to do with the concrete bases was less certain. When petroleum production ceases, the general rule is that the installations must be removed to land. Possible exceptions include concrete gravity base structures, particularly heavy steel jackets and damaged installations. Dumping structures in deep water is no longer an option, unless an exemption is made.

The options that were considered for *Frigg TP1* were either complete removal, dumping in deep water, cutting the concrete legs down to 55 meters below the sea surface so that sea traffic was not obstructed, or abandoning the facilities on site. This was the first time the UK government had to decide what to do with this type of platform, under the rules of the Oslo-Paris convention for the protection of the marine environment (OSPAR), established in Paris in 1992, ratified by Norway and most of the other west European nations, and brought into force in March 1998.

Frigg TP1, located between *QP* and *TCP2*, on the Frigg field – Bob Fleumer/Norwegian Petroleum Museum

OSPAR ruled: 'The dumping, and the leaving wholly or partly in place, of disused offshore installations within the maritime area is prohibited.' However, it recognised that there may be significant risks in removing large concrete structures and created a provision for owners to apply for exemption from the general rule of complete removal. This allows operators to leave gravity bases in place, either with the shafts intact or toppled, or to refloat and dump them in deeper water.

The concrete platforms at Frigg had not been designed with an eye to their removal and proved difficult to shift. Studies included several proposals for re-using the bases – such as artificial fish reefs, foundations for wind turbines or carbon-free gas-fired power stations. Experts also assessed possibilities for removing the concrete structures but warned that an accident while they were being refloated could have major consequences. The bases might collide and sink to the seabed in a damaged condition, such a scenario presenting a major safety hazard and high additional costs. Cutting off the tops of the concrete legs 55 metres below the sea surface was also considered but that was assessed to be even riskier than removal.

It the end it was decided to simply abandon the concrete platforms on the seabed where it stood, marked by beacons to alert vessels to its presence.

There was a similar dilemma facing Shell UK when it decommissioned *Brent Charlie* after the platform ceased production in March 2021, four decades after it was installed in the North Sea. The company initially opted to remove the 30,000 tonne topsides from the platform for reuse/recycling on land.

Shell studied various options for its Brent concrete bases (it had three to deal with including *Brent Charlie*), including underwater demolition in situ. Such a process had never been attempted offshore on concrete structures as big as the Brent ones and would require extensive subsea work by saturation divers and remote vehicles, heavy lift vessels and an extraordinary amount of offshore and onshore handling of small pieces of reinforced concrete. The company estimated that it would take at least a decade to dismantle and remove all three Brent concrete platforms, and that the associated levels of safety risk to workers would be considerably greater than the maximum levels generally deemed acceptable by the UK oil and gas industry. A high-level analysis of the time, effort and safety risks of such a programme ruled out this option as too risky and expensive.

Shell stated that the only realistic method for completely removing any of the Brent concrete structures would be to undertake a reversal of the original installation procedure. This would involve refloating them and towing them back to shore for dismantling and the recycling or disposal of material. The company engaged leading concrete platform designers, engineering companies and engineering consultants to examine in greater detail whether it might be technically feasible to refloat any of the Brent bases.

In addition, they also looked at how the bases would be disposed of once they were towed ashore. Options included completely dismantling them and then, in a dry dock, recycling all the retrieved steel and concrete (for aggregate or road base material), or removing the legs completely and recycling them, and then moving the caisson to another site and positioning it on the seabed as an artificial island.

Shell stated: 'The Brent GBSs are first-generation structures and although their design was at the forefront of technology at the time it took no account of the possible future need to remove them. The ability of the structures to resist the loads that might be experienced during refloat was not considered and no specific features were incorporated to allow for removal.'

After a significant investigation on the state of the structure, particularly on the condition of the systems built into the platform to aid its original installation, the company deemed that the amount and level of difficulty of the work required on *Brent Charlie* to make it safe to refloat rendered an attempted refloat an 'unrealistic prospect'.

'First generation concrete GBSs were not designed for refloat and no attempt has yet been made to refloat such a structure. Significant uncertainties would have to be overcome to address the engineering challenges involved in each of the steps leading to potential refloat. Many generic and installation-specific technical and engineering problems would have to be dealt with before any refloat could be attempted. Several systems would have to be refurbished or replaced. Some of the conceptual sub-programmes of work would require access to parts of the structures that were last accessed during their original construction.

'Crucially, despite the detailed levels of planning, design and testing that would inevitably be performed, some of the systems vital for a successful refloat – which includes not only the initial refloating offshore but also the tow to shore and the prolonged period of floating deconstruction – could only be absolutely proved and verified during a real attempt to refloat.'

Shell concluded that the option 'complete removal by refloat' for *Brent Charlie* was not considered to be tenable – the risk of failure was just too great – and began looking at two other options, including leaving the concrete base in place or partial removal, which would involve cutting off the four legs below the waterline. The latter was predicted to cost £48 million while simply leaving the platform in place, including capping the tops of the legs and installing equipment to warn vessels of its presence, was costed at £450,000.

Shell's preferred option for all three of its concrete platform bases in the Brent field, including *Brent Charlie*, is to leave them in place and estimates suggests while they will all slowly degrade and eventually collapse underwater, as salt water penetrates the concrete and corrodes the steel reinforcement, they could remain standing for at least the next 1000 years.

The last and largest of the three Ardyne Point platforms – *Cormorant Alpha* – was sold by Shell to the Abu Dhabi National Energy Company in July 2008 and was operated by its subsidiary TAQA Bratani Ltd. Production ended in late 2023 although decommissioning plans were submitted two years earlier and removal of the platform's topside is planned to start in 2025. However, the company has yet to decide how it plans to decommission the concrete platform base. In the meantime, TAQA pledged to remove any remaining oil in the caissons once the topsides had been removed.

Acknowledgements

The following are acknowledged as sources of information used in the writing of this book: *Aberdeen Press & Journal*, British Newspaper Archive, *Daily Record*, *Glasgow Herald*, *Glasgow Evening Times*, Google News Archive, McAlpine Sea Tank monthly reports to Elf, *Marine Week*, National Archives of Scotland, Norwegian Petroleum Museum, *Ocean Industry*, *Offshore Magazine*, *Oil & Gas Journal*, Shell UK, *The Scotsman* and *The Sunday Post*.

About the Author

James Carron is a freelance writer based in Scotland.

Contact jimcarron@gmail.com or visit jamescarron.wordpress.com

Other Books by James Carron

Portavadie and the Ghost Village of Pollphail

The landscape of Scotland is littered with lost communities, most emptied during the notorious Highland Clearances. But there was one abandoned village that dated from much later – the mid-1970s. It was called Pollphail and it was a legacy of the early optimism of the North Sea oil boom.

Mired in financial scandal and branded an expensive white elephant, it was for decades, prior to its demolition, an uncomfortable reminder of the cost of failure.

It differs from the historic lost villages of the Highlands and Islands, which were forcibly cleared of their residents, in that Pollphail was never occupied. No one ever lived here and there is no evidence to suggest anyone ever even spent a night under its roofs. The only long term occupants were the sheep, rabbits and bats that found their way in after the place was bequeathed to nature and the elements.

Located on the southern tip of the Cowal peninsula, on the west coast of Scotland, Pollphail was built at the taxpayers' expense amid the early days of the North Sea oil and gas boom. It was designed to house an army of migrant workers. But the men never came and, for over four decades, this fully equipped company town lay empty.

The reason was close at hand; less than half a mile away, at Portavadie, multi-million pound concrete oil platforms were to have been constructed in a vast man-made lagoon. But a sudden sea change left the venture high and dry. And the whole place was simply abandoned.

Fully illustrated with photographs, maps and plans, this history charts the rise and fall of Portavadie and Pollphail from the mid-1970s to the present day, exploring the reason why the project failed so spectacularly and the legacy it left in its wake..

Lighthouse Men & Women of the Moor

The signalmen and women and stationmasters of Rannoch Moor worked in such far-flung, isolated outposts that 'lighthouse men and women of the moor' seems a particularly apt title for them. They looked after Corrour Siding, Rannoch Station and Gorton Crossing, all three remote beacons for the early Victorian and Edwardian travellers who ventured across this barren wilderness.

Conditions were primitive, particularly in the early years. There was no electricity until the 1980s and, in the case of Gorton, no running water. Homes were heated and meals cooked with coal, paraffin lanterns and later batteries proffered lighting, and they relied on the railway for supplies, which in times of bad weather could be severely delayed, leaving cupboards bare.

But, when the time came to leave, they refused to go, such was their loyalty to the line and to the moor. It was a way of life that intrigued and often mystified passengers. Rather than simply offer up another history of the West Highland Railway, this book aims to tell their story.

Secret Scotland

Fifty unusual and offbeat attractions, quirky curiosities and hidden gems, secluded and less well-known spots that await discovery. Most can be visited at any time of the year, day or night, with no booking required or admission charged.

Highland Hermit – The Remarkable Life of James McRory Smith

James McRory Smith lived for over 30 years at Strathchailleach, one of the most remote cottages in the Britain Isles. The building sits alone in a vast tract of empty, featureless terrain to the south of Cape Wrath, in Sutherland. There is no access road, no running water, no electricity and no telephone.

Yet James McRory Smith survived here, battered by the elements and devoid of human company. His story is a fascinating account of a man pitting his wits against the wilderness, enduring endless isolation and existing, for a large part, off the land. James' lifestyle belonged to a bygone age, yet he lived it in the 20th century, turning his back on the luxuries and conveniences of the modern world.

Tin Tabernacles and other Corrugated Iron Buildings in Scotland

Corrugated iron is a common sight in industrial and agricultural buildings. Less common are the tin tabernacles, mission halls, hospitals, schools, houses and cottages constructed during the 19th and early 20th centuries. Derided by some, overlooked by others, those that remain standing to this day are legacy to a branch of architecture that dared to be different. Born of necessity, this black sheep of the building trade matured into a distinctive and delightful character of both the rural and urban landscape.

Charting the history of corrugated iron as a construction material from its earliest days in the 1830s through to the Second World War, this book explores the once thriving market for kit-built kirks, ready to assemble reading rooms and off-the-shelf schools that sprung up across Scotland, often in some of the most remote and far flung corners of the country. Inexpensive to erect and frequently regarded as a temporary fix, many of these quirky little buildings remain standing and in use to this day.

For more information on Amenta Publishing titles, available in both ebook and paperback formats from Amazon, visit amazon.co.uk

www.ingramcontent.com/pod-product-compliance
Lightning Source LLC
Chambersburg PA
CBHW070121230526
45472CB00004B/1354